LMYR.

DAILY AFFIRMATIONS

DANISHA BURNETT-BONNER

ARTWORK BY JORDAN WRIGHT

1.

I have a *power-ful* contribution to *make.*

I was put in this earth to make a difference. There is a need that only I can meet. It doesn't matter how big or small. As long as I do my part, it will make a difference. I will show up in every moment as if I were meant to be there, because I am!

2.

My

aggra-vation

will
become
my
motivation.
I ***will*** fix what
is frustrating me.

Instead of remaining frustrated, I will look for solutions.
I know they are out there and I will be diligent in
looking for them. I will not be powerless over my
problems but instead, I will use my energy to make
changes. Frustration will lead me to my future.

3.
The
world
is waiting for
me.

Despite all of the ideas, inventions,
and intelligence in the world, my
brilliance is needed. There is a place
for me and I will find my audience.
I will leave my mark on the world.
And the world will be better for it.

4.
I will have *every-thing* I need when *I need it.*

I will not fear scarcity. Good things are coming to me. I can give without worrying about lack. I can let go and know that what is needed will come to me. I will trust that if I don't have it, I don't need it.

5.

Every-thing

can be
a gift
if I *choose*
to see it.

While I may not enjoy every situation, there is value in every situation. I will look for the good and I will find it. Although it may not be immediate, I will take time to see what I have been given: the lesson, the opportunity, or the reminder.

6.

I will

re-mem-ber

who *I am.*

In a world where ideologies cloud reality and opinions can shape my perception, I will discover and develop who I am. I will remain true to my original design and hold to that through all of life's challenges and changes.

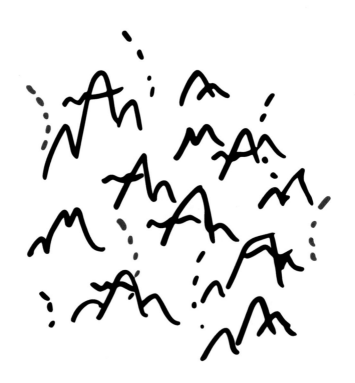

7.

I will
take a
chance.

Taking risks can be scary yet staying the same is scarier. I will not let the fear of the unknown paralyze me from my purpose. I will trust myself, my gifts and my abilities and move forward. I will leap and the net will appear. My destiny is worth the risk.

8.

I am *winning regardless* of how it looks.

Just as my experience is tailor-made, so is my victory. Not giving up is vital to my journey and the finishline is in view. As long as I stay the course, I will get there. I never lose; either I win or I learn and I will keep going.

9.

I will not let *fear* control *me.*

Moments may be challenging and I may feel afraid. Yet I will face those fears and keep moving. I am powerful beyond measure and can stand through what scares me. The goal is greater than my fears.

10.

There
is a
seat
at the table
for me.
If not,
I'll just bring
my own.

My gifts make space for me and I
will occupy every single inch. I will
accept the invitation to greatness. I
know where I belong and will boldly
make my way to the table.

11.

My *high-est* now is the **springboard** for my next.

All of my accomplishments are valuable and are the building blocks of my future. I have not seen all there is and there is much more ahead. I stand on the stairs of past successes as I rise to the next level of greatness.

12.

I
will
not
allow
my past
to define
me.

I will own that it happened but it will not own me. I will not hide from the history; instead I will face the future with courage as I create the life I desire. I still deserve goodness and I will not stop until I obtain it.

13.

I will *learn* from it and *let it go.*

I bravely approach each situation and evaluate my experience. I am open to the lesson and refuse to be stuck in fruitless cycles. I have the power and right to move on. I detach myself from any thing that is not life-giving.

14.

I am
well-loved.

I am a beautiful soul, created in God's image, worthy and deserving of love. There are people who love me and I will focus my attention on those who value me and release those who don't appreciate me.

15. Being different is *my super-power.*

No one in the world is like me and my existence adds flare. The world would be boring without me and I will not conform to fit in. I am needed just as I am. That's why I'm here.

16.

I *am* enough

Nothing else is needed to complete me. I am wonderfully and fearfully made. The gifts and grace that have been bestowed on me are exactly what is needed for any circumstance I find myself in.

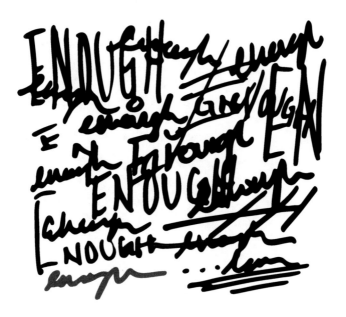

17.

I am
allowed
to
change.

As with every other creation,
I have the right to develop and
evolve. I am both a masterpiece
and simultaneously a work in
progress. Who I am today will be
different than who I am
tomorrow. Not only is that
acceptable, it is my aspiration.

18.

I am *deserving* of *love.*

I am God's highest design. My mistakes and failures do not disqualify me from love and happiness. I will accept nothing less than the best because I deserve it.

19.
My story *will* **inspire others.**

Shame will no longer plague my life. I will use my voice and my experiences to empower others. I will share what I have learned with all who will receive. Their lives will be blessed by my story.

20.

I ***don't*** have to figure it ***all*** out to start.

I am on my way to greatness; that's enough to begin. I will trust the process and not get lost in the details. Each step of faith will lead me to the next step. It will come together as I continue.

21.

I will
no
longer
wait to
be
great.

I came into this world equipped with all that I will need. I do not have to wait for the perfect conditions. I will appreciate the glory of the here and now and give the best of myself to this moment.

22.

I am
making progress,
even when
it feels
like
I'm not.

Where I am today is not where I was and tomorrow, I will be further along than today. I am doing better than I am giving myself credit for. I will keep going.

23.

I am
ready for
amazingly
different.

I will no longer stay in situations
that I have outgrown. I will
welcome change and embrace
each new opportunity, knowing
that I am prepared for the next,
best days of my life.

24.

My **_current situation_** is **_not my_** final destination.

I will not allow the details of my now to discourage me from reaching towards my next. I am on my way and I will not stop until I am there. I will make myself proud by finishing.

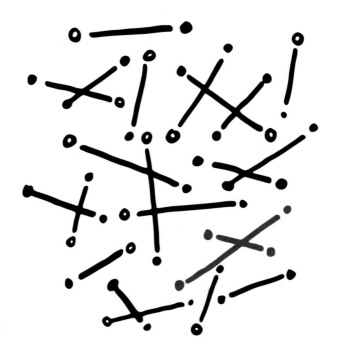

25.

While the situation is *not* ideal, I can *handle it.*

This may not be going exactly as planned but it is not insurmountable. I can adjust and adapt while staying focused on the goal. I have what it takes and will use my resources to successfully navigate every challenge I face.

26.

I will not compete against

anyone else.

This is personal. I will not compare myself to others; they are not racing me. I will devote my attention to my life. I will be inspired, not intimidated, by those around me. I will use their wins as encouragement.

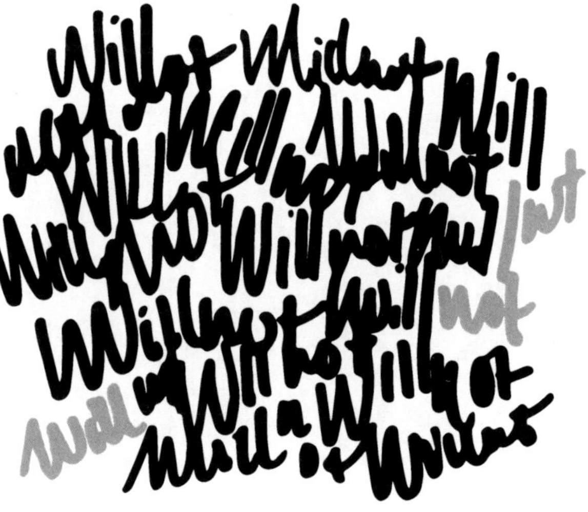

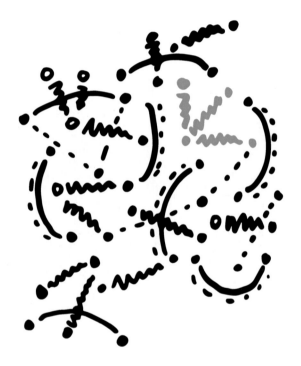

27.

I will bring God *glory* by being *fully me.*

The Creator wisely and carefully designed my every detail. I am an original- a once in an eternity. All of me brings glory to the Creator and I will not withhold any part. I am needed.

28.

I will *finish* what I *start.*

I will not allow distractions to divert my attention. I am focused on what matters and my efforts will be effective I am a finisher.

29.

I will **not** miss *my* *moment.*

I am prepared for greatness.
I am a part of Divine timing and
each experience has led me to
this moment. I will show up and
be fully present.

30.

I will *not fear* bad things happening.

I will only expect victory. The uncertainty of the future will not debilitate me. I will be aware but not afraid. I will practice radical acceptance and optimism. Hope will prevail.

31.

I will **_not_** **_stress_** over inconsistent people.

I will love them and still move forward. I will not allow myself to be hostage to their vicissitudes. I can keep going and allow them to catch up to me.

32.

I *love* who I am

be-coming.

I love me and am proud of my
journey. Each experience
contributes to my evolution and I
honor my process. I am a work of
art and a blossoming beauty.

33.

I *am* *stronger* than I think.

I have already survived 100% of my hardest days. I am a fighter and I have what it takes to continue and conquer. I am not weak but powerful beyond measure. My life shows my strength.

34.

I *am* *unstoppable.*

I am a champion, able to overcome every obstacle I face. The Greater One lives in me and enables me to always win. I defeat anything.

35.

I will *not* *fear* being wrong.

I can learn from my mistakes and will not allow shame to overshadow me. I am humble enough to be wrong and I will not stop trying. I will embrace failing as it, too, is an occasion to improve.

36.

I had a *pur-pose* *before* they had an opinion.

My life is not defined by what others think. I am not here to please them. I will choose what brings me satisfaction and honor my inner truth. I will honor my value and celebrate my worth daily.

37.

I will prior-itize myself.

Although I am a giver and am able to meet many needs, I will extend the same compassion and care to myself, as I am deserving. I will balance serving others with tending to my needs. Self-care is not selfish and I will freely care for myself without apology.

38.

I may struggle,

but I will

not quit.

Days will be hard but I am stronger. I will meet every challenge with courage and tenacity. I will not quit; instead I will gain strength in the struggle and emerge triumphant.

39.

I
am
light.

My light is internal and I will shine even in the darkest times. No one can extinguish the radiance of my presence and I boldly shine light everywhere I go, illuminating the path for others.

40.

I will *choose joy.*

My emotions are not in control of me. I have the power of choice and I will not waste energy on negativity. My outlook is my choice and I will adjust my feelings by changing my mind. I will set my heart on joy.